If We

Were All

#Financially

Literate ...

If We

Were All

#Financially_

Literate ...

49 *Virtues of Financial*

Knowledge

R. NELSON LETSHWENE

Published by:

Moedi Publishing

A division of Moedi Learning Technologies (Pty) Ltd;

PO BOX 80927, GABORONE, BOTSWANA

PO BOX 1766 RUSTENBURG, 0323, SOUTH AFRICA

Moedi Publishing

ISBN: 978-0-9870189-6-0

If We Were All #Financially_Literate

CreateSpace Publishing Platform on www.amazon.com

ISBN-13: 978-1523871902

ISBN-10: 1523871903

"The Light of God Never Fails!"
St. Germain

Disclaimer:

This publication is designed to provide competent and reliable general information regarding the subject matter covered. However, it is published with the understanding that neither the author nor the publisher are engaged in rendering legal, financial, or other professional advice through this medium. If legal, financial, or other expert assistance is required, the services of a professional should be sought. The author and publisher specifically disclaim any liability that may be incurred from the use or application of the contents of this book.

Dedication

To All Financial Knowledge Seekers

Also by R. Nelson Letshwene

1. *The Money Field* – in the game of money, all are players, but some are more skilled than others.
2. *Seven Essential Money Skills* – building a healthy relationship with your money.
3. *Your Longing Is Your Calling* – finding your purpose through the seven desires of life
4. *Faith and Purpose* – Living your life to the full without Fear, Guilt, or Regrets
5. *Functional Mastery Over My Finances*
6. *Mastery Over Debt – (Audio)*
7. *Financial Mastery Seminar – (Audio)*

For more articles visit the blog on
www.7moneyskills.wordpress.com *or*
www.nelsonletshwene.com

Table of Contents

Preface

The importance of Financial Literacy cannot be overestimated. The 49 virtues of financial knowledge written here are meant to be thought stimulators. This is certainly not an exhaustive list of all the things we would be if we were all #financially_literate.

They are meant to stimulate your thoughts to think more about any of these topics in a way that could be more practical for you. I started the thought process and I would like you to finish it off and apply it to yourself.

I wrote 49 because I know you can think of the 50th, the 51st, and beyond that. At the end of each of these there's space for you to expand on any of these thoughts with your own notes and thoughts.

We all need to stop and consider how our lives would change *If We Were All #Financially_Literate*. Let us stimulate the money conversation. Let us Twit about being #Financially_Literate and talk about these virtues on all social media platforms.

I am certain we can change lives by just stimulating

the conversation.

Nelson Letshwene

Gaborone, Botswana,

30th September 2016

Twitter handles:

@NLetshwene / @101silverline

Introduction

What is Financial Literacy?

"**Financial literacy**[i] is the ability to understand how money works in the world: how someone manages to earn or make it, how that person manages it, how he/she invests it (turn it into more) and how that person donates it to help others."

More specifically, it refers to the set of skills and knowledge that allows an individual to make informed and effective decisions with all of their financial resources.[ii]

Being financially literate puts you in charge of your personal finances. It allows you to be able to read all the money documents and papers that come your way. Everyone generates money documents. Money always leaves a paper trail wherever it goes. A financially literate person is able to let these documents communicate back to them. They can generate and read their own statements.

Let us start with some stats:

The Organization for Economic Co-operation and Development (OECD) published an international study in late 2005 analysing financial literacy surveys in OECD countries. A selection of findings[iii] included:

- In Australia, 67 per cent of respondents indicated that they understood the concept of compound interest, yet when they were asked to solve a problem using the concept only 28 per cent had a good level of understanding.

- A British survey found that consumers do not actively seek out financial information. The information they do receive is acquired by chance, for example, by picking up a pamphlet at a bank or having a chance talk with a bank employee.

- A Canadian survey found that respondents considered choosing the right investments to be more stressful than going to the dentist.

- A survey of Korean high-school students showed that they had failing scores – that is, they answered fewer than 60 per cent of the questions correctly – on tests designed to measure their ability to choose and manage a credit card, their knowledge about saving and investing for retirement, and their awareness of risk and the importance of insuring against it.

• A survey in the US found that four out of ten American workers are not saving for retirement.

What do these numbers tell us?

Are they telling us a story we are too familiar with? Are they articulating what we would not say with our own words?

Some might wonder about the fact that these countries are all first world countries. Are there problems of personal finance and financial literacy in all countries?

If first world countries with their resources are still battling with issues of financial literacy, what should third world countries do to start engaging the subject of financial literacy? Do we have enough material out there that could help people?

The fact that people don't actively seek out financial information, what could be done to get them interested in the existing material?

How many people will get this book and read it to the end? Will you?

49 Virtues of Financial Knowledge

1. BEING FINANCIALLY LITERATE

Financial literacy is the education and understanding of various areas of personal finance. Being financially literate is the ability to manage your financial matters in an efficient manner, and making appropriate decisions about personal finance such as investing, insurance, real estate, education funding, retirement planning, protection planning, tax planning, estate planning, and budgeting and debt planning.

Earning a high income does not necessarily mean that you are financially literate. Neither does earning a low income mean that you are necessarily financially illiterate.

Being financially literate is the ability to make sure that your numbers are congruent with your psychology of money.

The first step to making the right decisions is your ability to collect the right information about yourself. Everyone generates a paper trail. Money generates a paper trail. By gathering all your papers together, collating the information thereon and having a mirror of what your finances look like, allows you to make new decisions based on what you can see about yourself.

What is the story told by your paper trail? What are your

bank statements saying about you? What information do you find on your pay-slip? What are the bills on your table saying about your financial behaviour?

What are your investment statements saying about your assets? Have you drawn your balance sheet lately? Do you have a positive or a negative net worth?

2. ASK THE RIGHT QUESTIONS

If we were all #financially_literate, we would **know how to ask the right financial questions.**

There are people who never ask questions and just accept what "the experts" say. There are people who would like to ask question but do not have the knowledge base to ask those questions. Then there are people who ask wrong questions and therefore get inappropriate answers. The most important thing is to ask the right questions.

How would asking the right questions affect the world? What kind of financial decisions would each one of us make if we asked the right questions? What effect would those decisions have on our livelihoods? What effect would that have on the poor?

We would be more prepared in our lives for financial shocks. Would there be minimal financial shocks? Would the retirees of the world be living a better life? Would we be more prepared to educate our own children? Would student loans be as burdensome as they are today, especially in a world with seemingly shrinking job opportunities? What are the answers to these questions and what effect would they have in our lives?

Financial literacy would give us a base from which we would be able to ask the right questions. This would minimize criminals who prey on our ignorance.

What would you have to do to get yourself to a point where you can ask the right questions?

Sample Financial Questions To Ask

Every financial product has features and attributes. There are costs and there are benefits. The basic questions have to do with costs, benefits, and processes.

A loan product has four important elements around which you should ask question:

- How much is my loan amount?
- How much do I pay in instalments?
- What is my interest rate?
- How long will I pay for this loan? (term)
- What will be the effect on my loan if I vary any of these four; e.g. a change in interest rates, or a change in instalments?

An Investment Product has its basic questions:

- What is my growth projections for this product?
- What are the costs of this product
- Who is my fund manager and what are his qualifications or experience?
- Where will this money be invested?

- When will I get it back and how?

An insurance product has its attendant questions

- What does this product protect me against?
- What is the value?
- What are my costs?
- What are the claim procedures

For every product you buy, you need to know its attendant questions that lead you to making the right decision.

3. SEEK OUT FINANCIAL INFORMATION

If we were all #financially_literate we would **actively seek out financial information**.

What is financial information and where does one find it? Everyone who handles money generates personal financial information. Every transaction you do creates financial information about you. Beyond that, there is financial information about financial products and services.

If we were all financially literate, financial information wouldn't happen to us by accident. We would read more, listen more, and engage more. We would break the silence and talk more about finances. We would increase our financial vocabulary. We would actively seek out investment information so that we can actively grow our money. We would participate more in our financial education. We would not leave our fate in the hands of those who claim to be financial gurus.

We would actively peruse our financial contracts before we sign them. We would be interested in the paper trail we're all generating and seek to understand ourselves so much more better.

Start with the information you are generating. Can you read and understand your own paper trail? If you can't understand, your challenge is to seek that understanding by seeking more financial information that seeks to explain yourself to yourself.

Are you doing enough?

4. DRAW GREAT FINANCIAL PLANS

If we were all #financially_literate we would **draw great financial plans**.

Financial planning is about your total financial picture. It gives you a map of where you are going financially. Writing a financial plan is like writing your own financial policy. It will protect you against your own potentially bad decisions.

Most people are groping in the dark financially because they have never drawn a map of where they want to go. They have never drawn a functional long-term, medium term or short-term plan.

A holistic financial plan is made up of several sectorial plans. Many people don't even have the small plans to build up the big plan. They have never drawn *an investment plan,* so their money has no growth strategy. They go into debt without a *debt strategy* or *debt management plan,* so they end up working for other people, whose money they have consumed without a plan. They do not have a *protection plan,* so they remain vulnerable. They have never drawn a *wealth-building plan*, so wealth building remains a foreign concept.

The cliché applies to them: if you have failed to plan, you have planned to fail.

Financial success does not happen by accident but it happens by design. Once you have written a plan, lay the first brick.

5. A FUNCTIONAL RELATIONSHIP WITH MONEY

If we were all #financially_literate we would all have a **functional relationship with money**.

All things in our lives are in our lives because we have a relationship with them. A functional relationship, as opposed to a dysfunctional relationship, is based on mutual understanding. You have a relationship with money. Whether functional or dysfunctional, it's up to you to define.

Make money your friend not your enemy. An enemy is one with whom you are always at war, but a friend is one with whom you are at peace. Are you at war or at peace with your money? Are you in a cooperative relationship or are you dead set on destroying each other?

Have a true understanding of the value of money in your hands. It has been said that money makes a good servant but a bad master. Use money for its rightful purposes. Do not use money to control people or to hurt people, but to empower people. Give money direction, and it will serve you.

Along with the improved relationship we would have with money, we would have improved relationships with each other. We would know that money has its place in our lives besides other important things in our lives.

Do you have a functional or dysfunctional relationship with your money?

6. PROBLEM SOLVING SKILLS

If we were all #financially_literate we would have financial **problem solving skills**.

Every problem has a solution or the root of a solution within it. To truly solve a problem you must deal with its cause or source. If you only pluck out the fruit, without uprooting the three, at the right season, the fruit will show up again.

If we were financially literate, we wouldn't solve our financial problems with solutions that create more problems for us.

We would not be paying off debt with debt and thinking that we are getting out of debt. We would be rather seeking to expand our own means instead of relying on other people's money.

We would calculate and know the total cost of the problem. We would carefully check the recurring nature of the problem and not design half a solution. We would do proper brainstorming to come up with real solutions for our financial problems. We would carefully evaluate all possible solutions, weigh them against the problem, and choose and implement the most cost effective solutions.

At any given point, we would know that when we solve a financial problem, it would not rear its ugly head again. It would be solved for good. For this, we would be willing to seek help, and find it and use it.

Problems solving skills are a key to dealing with financial problems. Do you have such skills?

7. NOT EASILY INFLUENCED

"We eat the bread of charity because we are hungry. It revives, than it slays us"
Kahlil Gibran

If we were all #financially_literate, we would **not be bought off by dishonest leaders**.

Influence is a powerful thing. Whether you are influencing or being influenced, you need to be aware of the consequences of such influence. Being influenced is bad if it leaves our lives in a desperate condition. We get influenced when we give our power away.

Absolute power corrupts absolutely. Money is a great influencer in the hands of wrong people. If we are financially illiterate, we are vulnerable to being influenced easily. Power hungry politicians exploit the poor by "giving them charity" in exchange for power to rule over them. Why do the poor give away their power and allow others to rule over them? It is the perception that they cannot do anything for themselves, and that it is better if someone else does it for them.

A compassionate and generous society should take care of its own poor without exploitation. Politicians should lead the poor out of poverty through functional programs not disabling social grants. Even poverty alleviation programs should be economically empowering, not creating long term dependents.

If we were financially literate, we would not allow anyone to abuse people with our resources. We would stay true to our convictions and our hearts.

Who is influencing you and by what means?

8. BE TRUE TO SELF

"This above all, to thine own self be true"
William Shakespeare

If we were all #financially_literate we would **not be bought off by dishonest religious leaders**.

All growth costs money. This includes spiritual growth. But you cannot buy this growth with money. You need to work on it with all your body, mind, and soul. Being financially literate includes our relationship with our Higher Self.

Dishonest religious leaders often claim to have better contact with your Higher Self or your God than you do, and would like to "sell" this to you.

If we were all financially literate, we would know the difference between money used for "the work of God" and money used to enrich the religious leaders. We would demand more transparency for our monies at our places of worship without feeling guilty. We would be more proactively involved in the running of our religious institutions and activities instead of letting just one or a few people to run our lives in exchange for our money.

Never let anyone make you feel guilty about your money and your relationship with God. God is not for sale. Yes religion needs funds, but it does not need to defraud its people. We as a people would be vigilant and more "righteous" (right use) about how we use our money to fund our spiritual growth.

9. DIFFERENTIATE SAVING FROM INVESTING

If we were all #financially_literate, we would **know the difference between saving and investing**.

Saving and investing are two sides of the same coin. Without the one, the other wouldn't be. You save money so that you can invest it. We save for future survival, but we invest for growth. Saving is a stepping-stone to investing.

Not all saved money will be invested. Some will be consumed before it's invested. Some is saved for non-investing projects. Some is saved for emergencies. Money in a savings account does not grow as much as money in an investment account or investment system.

The purpose of investing is for growing our future money. We would deliberately grow our investments to ensure a comfortable future. We would learn more about investing so that we can genuinely grow our money.

Saving money is like generating seed money for investments. There are many investment platforms, but to save literally means to put cash aside. A portion of today's earnings must be set aside as savings so that it can be invested. Savings also helps with emergencies of life.

To invest fruitfully, you must acquaint yourself with investment systems. Such systems include stock markets, real estate, businesses, investment funds, etc.

Which investment vehicles are you using to grow your money?

10. CONTROL OUR EXPENSES

If we were all #financially_literate we would **control our expenses**.

All systems run through controls. Controls are only possible when there are objectives in place; otherwise they create havoc. If your objective were to reduce your expenses, you would need to put controls in place to achieve this objective.

Being financially literate would allow us to put functional control measures and management systems in our homes. We would not spend money and resources as if there is no tomorrow. We would curb all wasteful expenditure. We would define our needs vs. our wants. We would measure our resources to make sure that they meet our needs. We would throw away less food.

We would not clog our wardrobes with unworn expensive clothing. We would know when it's enough. We would not accumulate unwanted things that take our money and space in our lives as well as time and other resources. By putting these controls on our finances we would indirectly be affecting our health and our wealth. We would eat healthier and we would not be sick especially through stress.

11. SELF-CONTROL VS. SELF-REGULATION

If we were all #financially_literate **we would know the difference between self-control and self-regulation**.

Self-control has to do with our emotional involvement with our money. Without self-control we would live by our impulses. Emotions can bypass reason and move us to actions we would later regret.

Self-regulation is about putting measure in place to regulate the way we live our lives. Self-regulation is an understanding of ourselves through reason, and leading ourselves to our objectives.

Self-control is about the management of our knee-jerk reactions and our impulses. We would know if something is motivated by an emotion or if it is motivated by sound reasoning. Self-regulation is about setting money rules in place and living by them. Self-regulation is key to self-control. It is a guiding principles through which you sift your emotions. Every emotion can be measured against the money rules that you have set to meet certain objectives.

The first rule of money we would put in place is the "pay yourself first rule". Then we would add the control rule, and the investment rule, and so forth. We would self-regulate to our own success.

Are you controlled by your emotions or have you set rules to regulate your financial behaviour?

12. DISTINGUISH PRICES

If we were all #financially_literate we would **distinguish prices**.

Wants vs. needs. Necessity vs. non-essential. Beyond the most basic needs of food, shelter and clothing, who gets to say what is a need and what is a want? One man's need is another man's want. What is in a price? Does price tell us anything about needs and wants?

There is a very thin line between comfort and luxury; and yet the price difference between comfort and luxury can be double or triple. A luxury hotel can charge thrice the price of a standard hotel, with similar amenities offered. The ability to distinguish prices is really the ability to determine how much more you are willing to pay for an item or service.

A million dollar horse is only a fraction of a second faster than a ten thousand dollar horse. What is the price of that fraction and what is it worth for you? Why are you willing to pay that much more? Yes, we pay for tangibles and intangibles. We pay for physical realities and virtual perceptions. Does high price always equal high quality? Hardly! Does low price always equal low quality? Hardly. Do you always get what you pay for? The decisions are yours.

13. KNOW FRAUDSTERS

If we were all #financially_literate we would **not be defrauded by financial fraudsters.**

There is a difference between losing money in a fair deal, and being defrauded. Profit and loss exist in business because sometime you will make one and other times, the other. Being defrauded, however, is more painful than losing money in a fair deal.

Yes there are very "clever" fraudsters out there who are determined to defraud people. They do it electronically and physically. They may even have "evidence of success".

Being financially literate gives us an opportunity to read the deal fairly, and to know the difference between a scam and an opportunity.

So many pyramid schemes and Ponzi schemes have taken people's money away. We would also be aware of those who claim to be financial gurus but are not. We would be able to ask them the right questions and sift out the fraudulent from the real ones. We would have the eye and the mind to read the numbers and make informed decisions with our money. If something sounds too good to be true, it needs deeper scrutiny because it normally is. It is very important to know which questions to ask.

14. JOIN THE MONEY CONVERSATION

If we were all #financially_literate we would be able to **join the money conversation**.

When you find people speaking in a language you do not understand, you cannot join that conversation. Too many people are left outside the money conversation because they do have the vocabulary that allows them to speak about their money. Not having the right financial vocabulary leaves you out of the conversation. It is frustrating to have people speak to you in a language you do not understand. This happens a lot in finance. We get "talked to" instead of being conversed with. We sign in and participate in a game whose rules we do not fully understand.

Being financially literate begins to give us the vocabulary and allows us to speak the language of money. To this end we would read more personal finance books to gain more of this vocabulary and this language. We would actively seek out financial information. We would Google more articles about various aspects of money. Investopedia.com[iv] would be one of the websites we would frequent. We would converse about the good of money on our social networks. We would be able to strike a conversation with our children, our families and our colleagues.

Can you join the conversation right now?

15. READ FINANCIAL BOOKS

If we were all #financially_literate we would **read more financial books**.

If you do not know how to build a house, you go to the professionals to do it for you. The good thing about houses is that you only have to build it once.

Money, on the other hand, is not a once off subject. If you never learn anything about money, you will always have someone else making financial decisions for you. I'm not talking about daily bread and butter decisions, but important investment decisions on whose outcome your future depends.

It is not enough to make the excuse that you were not taught this subject at school. There are a lot of personal finance books now available.

If we read these would not be intimidated by the subject that is so important to our lives. Our homes would have more personal finance books. We would encourage our children to read more of these books. Most people stop reading by the age of 32, and yet they have to deal with money for the rest of their lives. If there's any area you shouldn't stop reading, it's the area of personal finance. Ignorance is not bliss. You don't want to reach your retirement age and still have other people making financial decisions for you. Keep reading books that give you the knowledge that will keep you in the driver' seat of your finances. Set a goal to read certain books per month. Never tire. Leaders are readers.

Have you read any of these?

Some Essential Personal Finance Books to Read

The following list of books is not exhaustive by any means, and does depends where you're at in your money game. To get further lists you can just search the internet to find more suitable books for you.

1. The Money Field – by R. Nelson Letshwene
2. Seven Essential Money Skills – by R. Nelson Letshwene
3. Think and Grow Rich – by Napoleon Hill
4. The Richest Man in Babylon – By George Clason
5. Money – Master the Game – by Tony Robbins
6. Why Didn't They Teach Me This at School – by Cary Siegel
7. The Millionaire Next Door – by Thomas J Stanly
8. Thinking, Fast and Slow – by Daniel Khneman
9. The Power of Habit – by Charles Duhigg
10. The Power of your Subconscious mind – by Dr Joseph Murphy
11. Rich Dad Poor Dad – by Robert Kiyosaki

16. PERSONAL FINANCE AT SCHOOLS

If we were all #financially_literate, we would have **personal finance at schools**.

Reading, wRiting, and aRithmetic – the 3R's, are the basics of what everyone who goes to school learns. A child will then pick to learn a skill based on talent and interest. Upon this, they will build their future career. From this career, they will earn a living, which will hopefully give them lots of money. What will they do with the money though? They have not learnt anything about financial management. Will they learn this skill from their parents? Yes they will, but unfortunately, most parents are learning by trial and error.

As a society, if we are serious about the success of our children and future generations, we would insist that our children should learn personal finance as the building blocks of their future. Everyone handles money but most people do not have money skills.

The teachers of our children would be able to teach basic financial literacy to our children. Currently, many of them are themselves in the dark and in many financial troubles, and therefore cannot teach this subject to our children. If we are determined to change the future of our children, we should give them financial literacy as a basic course in their lives. Can our children recognize financial documents? Do they know the difference between an invoice and a receipt? Can they read a statement? At what age do they enter a bank to transact?

If nothing else, we should give them the books to read for themselves, but we cannot postpone this any longer.

DID YOU KNOW?

Raising interest in personal finance is now a focus of state-run programs in countries including Australia, Canada, Japan, the United States of America, and the United Kingdom.

The Organization for Economic Co-operation and Development (OECD) started an inter-governmental project in 2003 with the objective of providing ways to improve financial education and literacy standards through the development of common financial literacy principles.

In March 2008, the OECD launched the International Gateway for Financial Education,[v] which aims to serve as a clearinghouse for financial education programs, information and research worldwide.

In the UK, the alternative term "financial capability" is used by the state and its agencies: the Financial Services Authority (FSA) in the UK started a national strategy on financial capability in 2003. The US Government also established its Financial

Literacy and Education Commission in 2003.

What are we doing in Africa?

17. MONEY CONVERSATION IN OUR HOMES

If we were all #financially_literate we would have the **money conversation in our homes**.

What dominates the conversations in our homes? The grades our children get at school? The sports they play? The neighbours? The latest TV program? Celebrities?

What should we be talking about that we are not talking about? Sex? God? Love? Money? Are we not talking about these because we don't know much about them or because we are embarrassed?

If we increased our knowledge on any of these topics, we would not be embarrassed at all. This book is about financial literacy so let's focus on money.

If we were financially literate, money talk would not be the taboo subject that it currently is in our homes. There would be more financially transparency in our homes. The silence around money would be broken. Everyone in the household would have a financial picture of what is going on.

The breadwinner wouldn't carry the load alone if everyone knew what was going on.

Monthly budgets would be discussed. Annual budgets would be drawn and discussed. Future financial goals would be set and discussed in the home. The level of household debt would be discussed. Everyone would discuss the family balance sheet and how to improve it.

What are you talking about in your home? Where to start? Choose one item. What is the price of a pint of milk? How many liters of milk are consumed in this house per month? Calculate the cost of that. Choose any item relevant to your household. Start the conversation.

18. NO FEAR OF MONEY

If we were all #financially_literate there would be **no fear of money**.

Most people will not acknowledge that they have the fear of money. But their relationship with money is characterized by fear. They have fear of spending; fear of investing; fear of giving; fear of acknowledging the presence of money.

Most people are uncomfortable in the presence of cash and they don't even know it. They have the impulse to spend it because they can't keep it in their pockets. The fear of money creates all sorts of imaginary scenes in the mind of the fearful person when they are in the presence of money. Their spending is driven by fear: fear that the price might go up if they don't buy now; fear that these items might run out if they don't buy them now; fear that the money might be used for something else if they don't spend it now; fear that someone else might steal the money from them; fear that it might be lost in an investment; fear in the presence of cash. They are so afraid to lose that they end up losing it. They are so afraid to hold it that they never have it to hold. The constant fear of money keeps people in a love-hate relationship with money. They long for it when it's not here, but when it gets here they are eager to get rid of it through expenditure. And then they long for it again, only to spend it again.

If we were all financially literate, we would have a healthy respect for money but not be fearful at all.

19. FUNCTIONAL MONEY BELIEFS

If we were all #financially_literate we would have **functional money beliefs**.

Belief is a powerful tool that shapes human life. Your life will always unfold in accordance with the beliefs you hold about life. Master Teachers like Jesus of Nazareth always said to his followers, "go it will be done just as you believed it would[1]".

Your belief or faith is so powerful that, because of Free Will, can even override God's will for your life! Life will always unfold according to your faith. So, be careful what you believe. Your beliefs are often articulated in your words. "Out of the overflow of the heart, the mouth speaks[2]!"

What you say with your tongue will become a reality in your life. We would throw away disempowering money beliefs such as "money is evil"; or "more

---

[1] Matthew 8:13

[2] Luke 6:45

money more problems".

Negative money beliefs influence our psychology of money negatively. Positive money beliefs help to grow our psychology of money. We would believe in the neutrality of money and would give it the right power through right beliefs. It is fine to believe that money grows on trees. That is the only way you will plant money trees. It is fine to believe that money can buy happiness, because when you have it, you just seem to be slightly happier than when you don't have it. It is fine to feel great about making money.

20. UNDERSTAND COMPOUND INTEREST

If we were all #financially_literate we would **understand the power of compound interest**.

"Compound interest is interest calculated on the initial principal and also on the accumulated interest of previous periods of deposit or loan"[vi]

It was Albert Einstein who said compound interest is "the greatest mathematical discovery of all time". He further said it should be called the eighth wonder of the world. Its wonder is in its ability to grow money exponentially. "Compounding is the process of generating earnings on an asset's reinvested earnings."[vii]

This, however, will only happen to those that are willing to allow compound interest to work for them. It only works for those who will give it seed money and time.

Understanding compound interest would develop the virtues of saving from youth. It would develop financial patience and persistence. It would get rid of the get rich quick mentality that impoverishes so many people. Compound interest is steady but sure. It works well with well researched investments run by credible professional investment houses and great financial products. Use it to your advantage.

21. UNDERSTAND CONSUMER DEBT

If we were all #financially_literate we would **understand the potentially enslaving power of consumer debt.**

It was Kahlil Gibran who said, "we devour the bread of charity because we are hungry; it revives, and then it slays us".

When you are desperate, debt may seem like charity. It revives; and then it slays you.

To borrow money for consumption is to enslave ourselves to moneylenders. It is to sell our energies off to moneylenders. Every cent that has been borrowed will obviously be returned with compounded interest accompanying it. Consumer debt shrinks our resources in the long term. As long as you are in consumer debt, someone else has an advantage over you.

What is the right use of debt? The wise only use debt to grow their own money, whereupon debt benefits both the lender and the borrower. But whether the borrower uses it well or not, the lender always benefits from compounded interest. It is up to the borrower to use borrowed money in such a way that they are better off at the end than they were in the beginning. That happens when borrowed money grows your own money.

It is not wise to borrow other people's money just to consume it.

22. DON'T BE CONFUSED

If we were all #financially_literate we would **not be confused by what financially literacy is**

Don't confuse the size of your income with whether or not you are financially literate. Earning a high income does not necessarily mean that one is financially literate. Neither does a small income mean that one is financially illiterate.

Personal finance and financial literacy are very important life skill subjects, and if you fail to pay attention to them, you will not fail to reap the reward of financial failure.

Don't confuse the size of your education with whether or not you are financially literate. Nicola Tesla[viii] was one of the greatest geniuses this planet has seen, with hundreds of patents to his name; and yet, "never having put much focus on his finances, Tesla died impoverished at the age of 86." Just as you should not confuse being a doctor with being healthy, don't confuse being an accountant, or working in a bank or financial services sector with being financially literate. Many in this sector are good at taking care of other people's money but not necessarily their own.

Don't confuse the size of your house, or your car, or your wardrobe, or other gadgets with being financially literate.

Don't confuse your popularity, fame, or the praise and accolades you get in the street with being financially literate. These may bring you money, but it does not mean you have money management skills.

23. IMPULSIVE SPENDING & RETAIL THERAPY

If we were all #financially_literate we would **understand impulsive spending and understand the dangers of retail therapy**.

We would understand our own impulses and bring them under control. Everyone, both men and women are impulsive spenders according to their own interests and impulses. The impulse to spend is triggered by the things you like the most. For things you don't like, this impulse is not triggered even if they are on sale. But the impulse to spend grows when things you like are paraded in front of you, especially at discounts. Know thyself. Know your triggers; know your impulses. Keep them in check. Mix your impulses with your rationality. When you're highly emotional, do not make a decision.

People who use retail therapy need a different kind of therapy. They go to the malls and get sucked in by the colours, the smells, the sights and sounds of the mall. They temporarily forget their life problems while they are spending their money. The mistake they make is they try to take the mall home with them. This requires lots of money. If they spend this money, and they go back home, they find that the problems that drove them to the mall still exist at home. Now they need psychotherapy which has been worsened by all that spending. There is no such fallacy as retail therapy. You feel good for a while, but then you have to face yourself again.

24. SET FINANCIAL GOALS

If we were all #financially_literate we would **know how to set financial goals**.

You can set your financial goals about how much money you want to make. You can also set financial goals about how you want to use your money or what your money should accomplish for you. The purpose of setting money goals is to give your money direction.

A portion of today's money must be sent to the future to accomplish a task for you. When you get to the future, you will only find in the future what you sent there today.

Setting a goal for Multiple Streams of Income (MSI) requires time and certain resources to be allocated to such an accomplishment. Decide on the number of income streams you would like to generate. How many revenue generating activities are you committed to today? In other words, what are you doing today that will generate an income for you?

Some people are still stuck in the past; that is, paying for things from yesterday that probably no longer exist. When you are in debt, you can also set a financial goal of getting out of debt by a certain time in the future.

So, your financial goals may start from yesterday, include today, and proceed to the future. All of these will be financed with today's money. The money you earn today will go towards debt servicing, some will go to wards today's living expenses, and some should definitely go towards assets and the future.

Do not live today like there is no tomorrow.

25. HIRE PURCHASE CONTRACTS

If we were all #financially_literate we would **understand hire purchase contracts**.

Businesses use hire purchase or rent-to-own contracts because they have tax benefits, and they use it to maximize the use of their cash flow.

At a personal level, hire-purchase contracts carry a different weight. Most people who participate in hire purchase agreements focus on two things only: the item they are buying and the monthly instalment they will be paying. They don't always look at the cash price vs. the total price at the end of the contract.

They don't always realise that they are actually borrowing money from the merchant.

Thus they don't ask about the interest on the borrowed money. If they realised this, they would come up with a good deposit, and arrange their own transport. They would read and scrutinise that contract before they commit. In most cases, the seller retains ownership of the goods until they are fully paid, and therefore has the right to repossess and resell to someone else in case of failure to pay.

While hire-purchase contracts may seem to help those who believe they can't save money, they would actually benefit more by creating the habit of saving money. The same commitment they make to hire-purchase contracts, they can make to saving money to buy these items.

26. KNOW HOW TO BUY A CAR

If we were all #financially_literate we would **know how to buy a car**.

Buying a car can be a strenuous process. Many people just focus on the model they want, and the installment they can afford. There are three people in this deal: you, the bank, and the dealer. Everyone is looking after their own agenda. Both the dealer and the bank are after the money. The dealer through price and the bank through interest. You are the only one interested in the car but you will be paying the other two. Don't take your eyes off the deal by getting lost in the car and its features. You need to understand the financing structure. Besides, once the deal is done, the bank still owns the car, until you can pay it off. Depending on the deal, the dealer may still be committed to the maintenance contract of the car. It is very important to scrutinize the deal to understand the conditions under which the dealer will not service the car. What is the cost of that maintenance contract?

The bank is interested in making sure "their car" is insured, but you are the one who will pay for it for the duration of the contract.

Consider the difference between a brand new car and a second hand vehicle.

Always consider the total cost of ownership. If you can afford the instalments, can you afford the insurance; the fuel costs; maintenance costs; protection costs (garage/locked gate) and all other costs.

27. KNOW HOW TO BUY A HOUSE

If we were all #financially_literate we would **know how to buy a house**.

More often than not, buying a house is a 20 to 25 year project. It is a decision that will be with you for most of your working life. The earlier you start the process the better. Your first house will not be your dream house, but by starting early, you can trade it off in the future for your dream house.

Most people don't qualify for the amount of loan that would acquire them their dream house with their earlier salaries, but they make the mistake of getting discouraged and not taking whatever loan amount the bank can offer. By the time they think they are ready to buy, their salaries are heavily committed to family responsibilities and to other life issues.

Even thought the mortgage contract may be for 20 years, by just paying an extra 10% on your mortgage, you could pay off your house in 10 to 12 years, depending on interest rates. This is using compound interest in your favour.

Being financially literate allows you to know all the options you can take to owning your home faster, and thus starting on your second property, or your dream home.

Read about mortgages and read about real estate and don't delay to participate.

28. KNOW HOW TO BUY FURNITURE

If we were all #financially_literate we would **know how to buy furniture**.

If you think you don't need financial literacy to purchase furniture, consider the number of repossessions and court cases going on based on hire purchase contracts gone wrong. Whether you buy your furniture cash or on credit, you need to consider other things like functionality? Draw your lines between comfort, luxury and decorum, and see the money gap between these. Draw your price lines. Remember, furniture gets used everyday so wear and tear and depreciation is high. You will be replacing this piece of furniture soon.

When you are still raising young children who will be jumping and spilling things on the furniture, or if you have indoor pets that will be all over the furniture, you need to decide how much money you need to use for such tools as furniture.

Luxurious furniture seems only appropriate when your children are fully grown and will not be jumping or playing on your expensive furniture. By restraining them from using this furniture, you may be creating some psychological blocks that you may not even be aware of.

Furniture is a tool that gets used in our homes on a daily basis. Apply financial literacy principles when you acquire it. Acquire the right piece at the right time.

29. FINANCE CHILDREN'S EDUCATION

If we were all #financially_literate we would **know how to finance our children's education**.

They grow up so fast, we say, and with each year that they grow, the cost of education keeps going up. Education funding is what should be entrusted to the power of compound interest. You need to contribute while they are still young and you need to keep doing it. This is the one saving and investment process that needs your commitment. Do it now, do it always. They will thank you that you did.

You can't leave it to politicians or to chance. You can't be distracted by today's needs and pressures. You need to make it one of your most important money rules and obey that rule.

If they are already going to school, don't just focus on today's fees, know that they will be in school until they are 22 or 24 years old. How many more years will you still have to pay?

If you have not done anything thus far, search for scholarships, bursaries, government assistance programs, and scrutinize student loan programs. Is there a well-researched income generating project that can pay your children's school fees? Is there a project that needs to be put on hold now?

This is a social investment that if we don't do it, we are indirectly creating a financial burden for our future self or for the government. Not to say anything about denying the children the opportunities to reach their potentials.

30. FINANCING OUR PROJECTS

If we were all #financially_literate we would **know how to finance our projects**.

Many projects go unfinished. Some people just start projects without doing due diligence. They start because right now they have the money to start. But they have not thought about the money to finish. Some start because they are driven by their emotions, but still, they have not done the full budget for the project. Some start, and along the way they get derailed because they did not foresee other things that could potentially derail their projects. Those who do due diligence, set aside the funds and all other resources to finish their projects, and they accomplish this successfully. They plan the details, they are patient, and they are persistent and never get discouraged.

Almost every project you embark on will need financing. This may be further studies, having a child, a house, a business, or a journey.

By doing prior research on the overall costs of a project, helps you to decide when you should embark on it, and how much you will need. You can then decide on your financing model or structure. How much debt will you use, and how much of your own saved money will you need? If you use debt, who will pay it back and for how long? What is the cost vs. benefits ratio?

31. BUILD TRUE VALUE

If we were all #financially_literate we would **build true value**.

The Money Field[ix] has four quadrants: Income, Assets, Expenses, and Liabilities. The Income quadrant is a measure of your productivity as determined by your income. Your Expenses quadrant is the measure of how much of your money goes to other people. Your Liabilities quadrant measure how much of other people's money is in your hands. The only quadrant that measures your true value is your Assets quadrant. Which quadrant are you most focused on? How much value have you built over time?

Most people start working at the age of 25 and aim to retire at the age of 65. That is a total of 40 years of work. It seems to be wrong to work for 40 years and have no real value at the end of that. It seems to be wrong to be sixty-five years old and still not understand how money works, after working for it for forty years.

Being financially literate could take care of all of that. While there are many reasons why people can be broke at the age of sixty-five, being financially illiterate should not be one of them. Value is built over time by those who will periodically examine their progress. They would take corrective measures and continue building wealth and resources. As time ticks along, they make tangible progress.

32. UNDERSTAND GUARANTEES AND WARRANTEES

If we were all #financially_literate we would **understand guarantees and warrantees**.

Every time you purchase an item of value it comes with a certain level of factory guarantee that it should do or perform what it was meant to perform within the guarantee period. For example, most electronics guarantees will exclude "damage by water or by falling". They are essentially guaranteeing only the "software" and not the hardware. Read your *guarantee* documents before you purchase additional *warrantee*.

Buying extended warrantee from the sales person at the shop may actually be a waste of money because that does not extend the useful life of that item. The additional warrantee from the shop may also exclude the same exclusions of the guarantee. So what are you buying?

You are buying a repair contract. The person who might be contracted to fix it for the shop might not be the manufacturer. There may be additional charges for "parts" not covered by the warrantee.

They take your money upfront, but at the end, you might still be inconvenienced. You might end up wanting a new gadget anyway and not want to repair the old one.

A warrantee is not an insurance contract. They won't replace your item if it's lost. If you replace it yourself, your warrantee may be tight to the serial number of a lost item.

33. UNDERSTAND SHORT TERM INSURANCE

If we were all #financially_literate we would **know how to purchase short term insurance**.

Every asset you have is valuable to you because you spent your money to acquire it. The loss of any valuable thing can set you back for years.

Insurance gives you the ability to replace your valuable items in case of loss. This loss can be through theft, fire, or other damages. By paying a small contribution, you protect yourself from having to buy the item again at its full price should it be lost or damaged.

When we are not insured we remain vulnerable. We can insure movable and immovable property such as a house. The importance of home owner's insurance is that it protects the structure at its replacement value.

We face risks every day that we need to be insured against. For example, every single home uses fire every single day, whether in real form or as electricity. Just one spark could set the house alight. This risk is insurable.

Make sure you revalue your items every year so that you do not pay more than you should in insurance, because the insurance company will only pay you the current value at the time of loss. Understand your insurance policy and be clear about what is covered and what is not covered. Don't find out when it's too late.

34. TOTAL COST OF OWNERSHIP

If we were all #financially_literate we would **understand the total cost of ownership**.

There is a price for buying at item, and there is a price for owning an item. Total cost of ownership includes all costs associated with the item such as the price, maintenance costs, protection costs such as insurance and storage like parking garage for a car, and running costs such as fuel, tyres, cleaning, etc.

Most things that we own, including pets and air conditioning units, have a cost of ownership. Understanding total cost of ownership takes us back to the decision table where we decide whether to own something or not. It is not enough to have money to buy it. You must have money to own it also. You must include in the price, all the costs that you will incur over the life of the item.

Price is a fraction of the cost. Total cost of

ownership is the real cost of owning an item.

Before you make the next buying decision, sit and calculate all the costs associated with that item – from dry clean costs, to dog food, to extra electricity costs to your air conditioning unit, to rates and taxes for your home, to maintenance costs and running costs.

35. SET MONEY RULES AND LIVE BY THEM

If we were all #financially_literate **we would set and live by money rules.**

Money rules give us an opportunity to create functional habits with our money. Money rules may seem hard in the beginning, but if you keep up with them, they will become your habits, and you will be glad that you set these rules.

In the spirit of George Clason's classic, *The Richest Man in Babylon*, set rules such as:

(1) the "pay yourself first rule". This rule will direct you to make sure that each time money comes to you, you set aside at least 10% for your wealth building programs.

(2) Control your expenses. If uncontrolled, they erode your wealth.

(3) Invest your money profitably and regularly

(4) Set processes to own your home as fast as possible

(5) Save for your retirement as early as possible, and keep doing it.

(6) You can also set debt ratio rules; protection rules; investment rules; sharing rules; and all other rules that will guide your relationship with money. These ensure that your money is not unruly, but follows your leadership.

Money rules are not meant to enslave you, but to help you to lead your money.

36. SAVE FOR RETIREMENT EARLY

If we were all #financially_literate **we would save for retirement early**.

Life journey can be so long and so rigorous that you might think retirement would never come. As surely as your child is ten years old, you too have added ten years to your life since the birth of that child. Many people are distracted by the idea that they will land a big deal that will take care of their retirement. It is better to be sure now. Start contributing to a retirement fund as early as you can and keep doing it through thick and thin. Let compound interest do the wonders for you. If your big deal comes, you can always use more money in retirement. But if your big deal never comes, you will be glad you have something to live on.

Retirement funding is very important, because of all the investment schemes out there, it is the only one that the government is willing to protect and encourage you to do. Your contributions to your retirement are tax deductible up to very generous limits in many countries. So, if you want to reduce your taxes, increase your contributions to your own retirement fund or pension.

A pension fund is also protected against insolvency, so the policy cannot be used as collateral for a loan. A pension may also be inherited by your heirs.

DID YOU KNOW?

"Research in the US shows that workers increase their participation in retirement planning[x] when employers offer financial education programmes, whether in the form of brochures or seminars."[xi]

37. UNDERSTAND THE STRUCTURE OF DEBT

If we were all #financially_literate we would **understand the structure of debt**.

Debt is not just the idea of taking other people's money and returning it over time in instalments. Many people are overburdened and are actually stuck in debt because they just don't understand the structure of debt.

Each debt is made up of four elements: the amount, the instalment, the interest and the time. Each one of these factors affect the others.

Most of us are only interested in the amount of the loan. But we have to examine all of the other elements.

When your instalment goes down, it is only possible when time goes up, and along with it, the amount you will end up paying.

When you increase your instalments, you reduce the time it will take you to get out of debt.

Interest is the price you pay for "other people's money", or debt. Money is not free.

Many people have spent many years in debt because they never process the "time element" in debt. By consolidating a loan, you are essentially extending the time it will take you to get out of debt.

The only fast way to get out of debt, is to increase your installments, not reduce them. Reducing them may give temporary relief, but it keeps you a prisoner for longer.

Take some time and understand debt. (I have devoted the entire third section of my book *The Money Field*[3]–, to understanding debt.)

---

[3] https://www.amazon.com/Money-Field-Everyone-Player-skilled-ebook/dp/B00UBR7460/

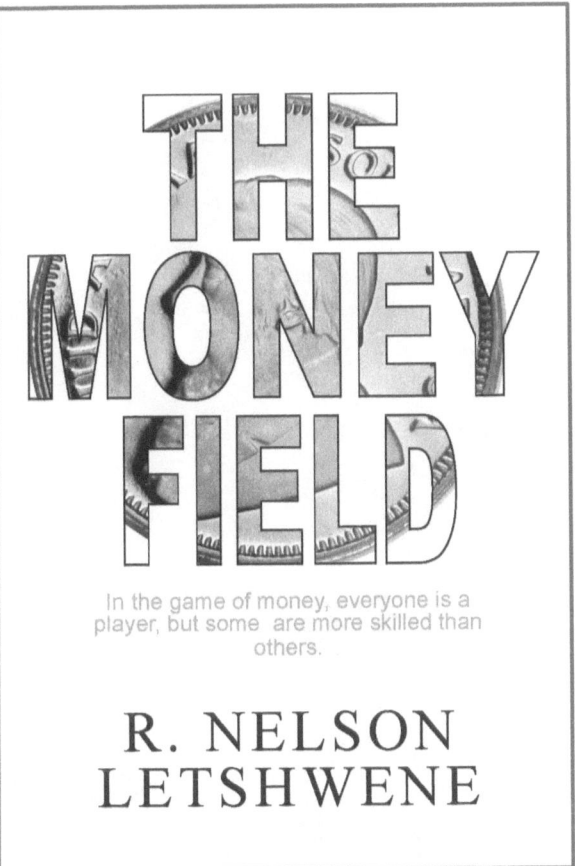

https://www.amazon.com/Money-Field-Everyone-Player-skilled-ebook/dp/B00UBR7460/

38. UNDERSTAND LIFE INSURANCE

If we were all #financially_literate we would **understand life insurance products**.

As long as you have people that are depended on your active financial muscle, as opposed to passive income, life insurance is a very important necessity.

Passive income is money coming to you without you actively going to work. Such income can be Willed to your dependents. Active income, however, is income that is dependent on you going to work for it. If you don't work, it does not come in.

Should you lose your ability to support them financially, either through death or disability, life insurance can be that financial person that kicks in to take your financial responsibility. There are various types of insurance covers to explore. There's life insurance; there's disability insurance; there's dread disease insurance; there's accidental death cover; etc.

Because it is an item that is dependent on your health, it is important to understand what the insurance company requires you to disclose about your health and what is automatically covered. If you wait until you need it, it might be too late. Get covered early. And make sure that the cover is sufficient.

39. BALANCE THE BUDGET

If we were all #financially_literate we would **be able to run a balanced budget**.

"If your outgo exceeds your income, your upkeep, is your downfall"

Writing a budget goes far beyond just stating what you are going to spend your money on. The real budget is a tool that helps you to also focus on your ability to make more money. A budget is not only a control tool, but it is also a forecast and focus tool. It allows you to control the present and forecast the future.

It is important to live within your means, but it is much more important to expand your means than to try to fit within your means. The fact is, your life is not static. Your life is expanding. As you grow older or your children or dependents' needs change, your income needs to be on a trajectory that will always meet your needs. If it's static, there will obviously be problems.

A positive budget allows you to spend considerable amount of time and resources on revenue generating activities instead of just controlling expenses.

To have a positive budget is to rather make sure that you run a surplus budget instead of a deficit budget. At worst, have a balanced budget. A deficit means you are either living on other people's money, or you are projecting to do so.

40. CASH IS KING

If we were all #financially_literate we would **understand the value of cash as king**.

Cash must always be seen as an asset, instead of a tool that is used to acquire things. As long as it is seen only as a tool, it will always be spent on sight. As soon as it is recognized as an asset that can help you to acquire more assets, it will be valued and treated differently. It will be treated with the respect it deserves.

Cash can be grown in liquid products or "near cash" tools such as money market funds, unit trusts, the stock market, or cash in a bank account.

Having cash on hand protects you from being vulnerable to emergencies that may force you into debt.

Buying things for cash is a challenge in a society that is used to living on debt. It takes great patience and discipline to raise the cash for the things you require in life instead of just swiping the credit card or taking a loan.

Even though saved money may earn little interest,

borrowed money takes a whole lot more interest from you. If you rely on debt, you will lose more of your cash to the interest charged by money lenders. You must also remember that lay-by is also cash. You don't get to pay interest and you will eventually have your items.

Reserve debt only for projects that will help you to make money instead of using debt to live your life. That is very costly.

Let your cash be the king that gathers more of its kind to you, and help you to rule your world.

41. UNDERSTAND THE STOCK MARKET

If we were all #financially_literate we would **understand the stock market**.

On any well-developed stock market, there are a lot of products and services up for sale. There are shares, exchange traded funds (ETF), bonds, and all kinds of derivatives. You don't have to know all of these to participate in the stock market.

The stock market allows you to invest in the companies that grow your own economy. You benefit as these companies grow and declare dividends. You also benefit from the capital appreciation of your shares, which you can turn around and sell to other investors.

Because companies use the stock market to raise funds for growth, this allows the public to directly participate in economic growth and get wealthy even as these companies build wealth.

If you know how to participate, and understand the

basics of what makes the prices go up and down, you can begin to learn as you participate. Your broker is your companion on this journey.

By getting a book on stock market trading 101, or stock market for dummies, or an idiot's guide to the stock market, you could learn a whole lot more than a person who assumes they know, and yet know nothing. These kinds of books offer the basics of financial literacy that we all need.

42. NETWORK MARKETING

If we were all #financially_literate we would **understand network marketing**.

Network marketing organisations, also called multilevel marketing (MLM), are companies that sell their products and services through a network of sales groups that promote these largely by word of mouth and group meetings. Sales agents are encouraged to build a network of people that will be the primary consumers, and secondarily sell to other people who are not yet members of these networks.

People are incentivized to join the groups through member discounts, commissions, bonuses and titled positions.

You must understand that these commissions and bonuses will only accrue depending on the amount of goods and services that are bought through your group or network.

They have a very high attrition rate. Many people

just don't know the amount of work it's going to take to be successful. Some network marketing companies have complex structures and offer no education while others will offer you business education and support.

You are taught that your group, or your network is your business and you need to run it like one. You need to study them very carefully, and to measure them against your own work ethic, skills, talents, and expectations. The fact is, money is made from the sale of products and services. If you can't sell, and your people skills are low, your chances of success in network marketing is close to zero. If it's not working for you no matter what you do, perhaps it's not for you.

43. PSYCHOLOGICAL CONUNDRUM

If we were all #financially_literate we would end **the psychological conundrum that separates us from money**.

Everybody relates to money at two levels: the numerical side and the psychological side. The numbers tell you how much money you have, and the psychological side is your emotional engagement with your money.

Your level of comfort or discomfort in the presence of money will determine how much you gather or scatter. Those with a high level of comfort in the presence of money gather more of it, while those with a high level of discomfort in the presence of money, scatter more.

People who ask wrong questions about money get wrong answers. Those who see money only as a tool, often get rid of it in exchange of the things they believe that they want.

They often ask, why should I suffer or be bored when I have money? They assume if their money went away (through spending), their suffering or boredom would go away. So they spend money, and still, they experience new kind of suffering and boredom.

Money does not have to go away for you to end your suffering. To have fun, you don't have to get rid of your money.

We need to end this conundrum, and understand that you can have both fun and money. They are not mutually exclusive.

44. TEACH OUR CHILDREN MONEY SKILLS

If we were all #financially_literate **we would teach our children right skills about money**.

Children don't learn at home like they learn at school. You don't need to put them in a class and lecture them. Life skills are learnt on the go. Swimming teachers don't put children in a class and teach them the laws of buoyancy and floatation before they put them in the swimming pool. They get with them in the pool and teach them to swim.

Most people learn their money skills by copying others. Your children will also copy you. So, you are already teaching them money skills. They learn by observing you. (Monkey see monkey do). How did you teach them your home language? You did not lecture them. You just went about your own business, and they observed and learned. They are currently learning everything you do about money.

If you are financially literate, they will learn money

skills from you, but if you are not, they are also learning that from you. What are you teaching? Wealth habits or poverty habits? The onus is on you.

The best way to change the course of your children is to change your own course. Encourage them to read personal finance books by making them available in the home. Together watch tv programs or radio programs that teach about money. Listen to audio programs in the car. Read together. Change together.

45. DON'T KEEP UP WITH THE JONES'

If we were all #financially_literate we would **not be trying to keep up with the Jones**'.

"Don't spend money you do not have, to buy things you do not need, to impress people you do not like."

There are a lot of things you do not know about your neighbours and there's a lot of things they don't know about you. We can almost be certain that you don't know a lot about their finances. The idea of trying to keep up with your neighbours is absurd because you don't know their financial models and financial structures. Neither do they know yours.

Financing a lifestyle with debt just to keep up with your colleagues, neibhours, friends – the Jones' – is to dig a grave for yourself while you're still alive.

You should just focus on your own financial game. Set your own goals and measure yourself against yourself, not against opponents you know nothing about. You might be following a shadow of the Jones's while their reality is different from what you see.

This kind of competitive behavior is rooted in falsehood, pride, and is egotistical because it is not based on equal measures.

46. SEEK FINANCIAL ADVICE FROM PROFESSIONALS

If we were all #financially_literate we would **seek financial advice from trained professionals**.

Just about every wealthy person in the civilized world has, either a wealth manager, a portfolio manager, a financial planner, or an accountant, and they have a real relationship with their banker. These are the money professionals.

You have medical professionals to consult about your health. When you have a legal problem you consult a lawyer. When you build real estate you call an architect and other construction professionals.

If you take your advice in any field from people who are not professionals in that field, you are very like to suffer losses. More so in the world of money. This is not a field you can leave to chance. Don't confuse a person's experience in any other field with competency in the field of money.

If we were all #financially_literate we would see the value of the money professionals. They have been taught the ins and outs of money. They know the laws that govern money from taxes to pension laws. Go to them for their knowledge. It doesn't matter whether they are practicing what they preach or not. Get their knowledge and put it to good use. You don't have to be rich to seek advice from a money professional. In fact, you need one to help you to build and to protect your wealth.

47. ENGAGE IN INCOME GENERATING ACTIVITIES

If we were all #financially_literate we would **focus on income generating activities**.

The financial goal of getting a job is to generate an income. The goal of a business person selling stuff is to generate an income. We generate incomes in many varied ways. Unfortunately some people think the only way to generate an income is through a job. People who think like that often get stuck without money because they are looking for a job instead of an income generating mechanism.

It is important to focus more on expanding your means than on trying to fit in within your means. If every day you did one thing that could potentially increase your income, either in the present time or in the future, life would be improving every day. Income generating activities are those that will eventually increase your means. They are different from income consuming practices.

You generate income by exchanging your energies, labour, your time, your skills, your talents, or your resources. Activities that will lead to income generation are marketing, promoting, and selling more of what you are currently selling. Everyone is currently selling something. Do something everyday, beyond just going to work, that will potentially increase your income.

Expand your means, and you will not have to worry about living within your means.

48. STOP HOARDING

If we were all #financially_literate we would **stop hoarding useless things in our lives**.

"The easiest definition of hoarding is when the amount of acquired clutter prohibits functionality in the home[xii]." Hoarding has various levels of severity from level one to level five.

Hoarders are those who gather stuff that may have been useful at some point in their lives, but they think it might still be useful again in the future, even though the evidence might suggest otherwise.

Hoarders have a hard time letting go of anything that they possess. One of the problems hoarders have is a scarcity mentality with an inherent fear of not having things.

Sever hoarding is a psychological problem and requires professional attention. If you suspect that you could be a hoarder, you can visit www.hoarders.com to learn more.

Functional frugality is important in that it helps you

not to be wasteful, but hoarding is dysfunctional behaviour in that you hold on to things that may have no value in your life, and end up clogging your life, not allowing new things to come in because you have no space for them.

It is important to do spring cleaning each year to differentiate the useful things from the useless things in your life and to get rid of clutter.

49. BE MORE GENEROUS

If we were all #financially_literate we would **be more generous**.

True generosity belongs to those who do not have the scarcity mentality. It is a feature of those with the abundance mentality. They don't have to be physically rich, but in their minds and hearts they are. True generosity is not laced with reciprocity. It is not covered with the "what's-in-it-for-me" mentality. It has no selfish expectations but only deliverables that make the recipient expectant with hope. True generosity is about meeting the needs of your fellow man, to lift him or her up to remember who they truly are. It is about making life better for another, that they may make their own life better. It is sharing your joy with others that they may be joyful, which will cheer others up.

It does not generate dependency in its wake. It does not leave people crippled where it's been but it leaves people empowered. True generosity awakens the sleeping giants within its recipients. It is the proverbial ability to teach a man how to fish rather than to supply them with fish.

True generosity is only a seed of fortunes planted within the recipients, which, when planted, will produce a harvest that obliterates lack and poverty.

50. If we were all #financially_literate ...

This is yours to complete:

_____

_____

_____

_____

_____

_____

_____

_____

_____

_____

_____

_____

RECOMMENDED READING

1.   ***The Money Field*** – *In the Game of Money, All are players, but some are more skilled than others*; R. Nelson Letshwene, Moedi Publishing, 2015

2.   ***Seven Essential Money Skills*** – *Building a Healthy Relationship with your Money*; R. Nelson Letshwene, Moedi Publishing, 2015

3.   ***The intelligent Investor*** – *the definitive book on value investing*; Benjamin Graham, Harper, 1973 (Revised Edition)

4.   ***Seven Spiritual Laws of Success*** – a practical guide to the fulfillment of your dreams; Deepak Chopra, Bantam press,

5.   ***The Trick to Money is Having Some***; Stuart Wilde, Hay House, 1998

6.   ***Who Moved My Cheese*** – An Amazing way to deal with change in your work and in your life; Dr. Spencer Johnson, Vermillion, 1998

7.   ***Money*** – Master the Game. 7 simple steps to financial freedom. Tony Robbins

Before Your Go ...

OTHER BOOKS BY R.Nelson Letshwene

LOOK out for these in the Kindle store and on www.amazon.com or on www.createspace.com/5069768

1. The Money Field – In the Game of Money, everyone is a player, but some are more skilled than others.

THE MONEY FIELD covers:

The Dimensions of Money; Your relationship with money; The Triangular Code; The Money Field; Rules on the Money Field; Debt and Financial

Intelligence; Financial Goals; Living in the Gap; The Personal Money Tree; Creating Records; Debt Management Systems; Debt The Four Elements of Debt; and Reduction plan.

2. Seven Essential Money Skills – Building a Healthy Relationship with your money

This covers The Seven Essential Money Skills being: Increasing Earning Capabilities; Saving Principles; Investing Systems; Building Value; Protection; Control Systems; and Sharing.

3. Your Longing Is Your Calling – How to Find your Purpose through the Seven Desires of Life

This covers the Seven Desires of life being: The Desire for Good Health; The Desire for Love; The Desire for Fulfilment; The Desire for Satisfaction and Self-Expression; The Desire for Joy; The Desire for Prosperity; and The Desire for Peace.

4. Faith and Purpose **– Living Life to the Full without Fear, Guilt, or Regrets**

This covers the Essential Elements of Faith being: Faith and Intuition; Tools of Knowing – Experience, Feelings, Thoughts, and Words; Dealing with Doubt; Surrender; Faith and Purpose; Faith and Actions; and The Science of Faith.

About The Author

Nelson Letshwene is a personal finance professional, a speaker and author on personal finance issues and personal development. He has been involved in personal finance and personal development training for over two decades.

He graduated from The University of the Witwatersrand (Wits) and from The University of South Africa (UNISA) with business degrees and continued to study and practice personal financial management through training and consulting. He is the managing director of Moedi Learning Technologies.

His amazon page is http://www.amazon.com/R.-Nelson-Letshwene/e/B00Q4AEMCM/

He is a blogger on:

www.7moneyskills.wordpress.com

For more information you can also visit his website:

www.nelsonletshwene.com

Follow him on twitter here @101silverline or @NLetshwene

His facebook page here :

(https://web.facebook.com/Money-Skills-with-NelsonLetshwene-452066951536749/)

End Notes

[i] https://en.wikipedia.org/wiki/Financial_literacy - *Giesler, Markus; Veresiu, Ela (2014). "Creating the Responsible Consumer: Moralistic Governance Regimes and Consumer Subjectivity". *Journal of Consumer Research* **41** (October): 849–867.

[ii] "Get Smarter About Money Home – GetSmarterAboutMoney.ca". www.getsmarteraboutmoney.ca

[iii] "Hecklinger, Richard E. Deputy Secretary-General of the OECD speaking January 9, 2006 at The Smith Institute, London". New Statesman. June 5, 2006.

[iv] www.investopedia.com is a website with lots of financial education and articles.

[v] "International Gateway for Financial Education > Home". www.financial-education.org

[vi] https://index.investopedia.com/index/?q=compound%20interest&o=40186&qo=investopediaSite Search

[vii] http://www.investopedia.com/university/beginner/

viii Nicola Tesla (10 July 1856 – 7 January 1943) was an inventor, physicist, mechanical engineer, and electrical engineer. Contemporary biographers of Tesla haved deemed him "the man who invented the twentieth century" and "the patron saint of modern electricity" – -Reference: http://www.world-mysteries.com/dougy.htm

ix See The Money Field, by R. Nelson Letshwene, Moedi Publishing. Also available on www.amazon.com

x 401(k) plans - a type of retirement plan, with special tax advantages, which allows employees to save and invest for their own retirement

xi "Hecklinger, Richard E. Deputy Secretary-General of the OECD speaking January 9, 2006 at The Smith Institute, London". New Statesman. June 5, 2006.

xii www.hoarders.com